I WOULD LOVE TO KNOW
YOUR OPINION.

THIS BOOK HAS BEEN AN
APPROACH TO THE FUNGI
KINGDOM, THROUGH DRAWING
AND FICTION, ONE OF MANY
WAYS OF LEARNING.

I HOPE THAT COLORING
AWAKENS YOUR CURIOSITY.

IF YOU HAVE THE
OPPORTUNITY TO COMMENT
I WOULD GREATLY
APPRECIATE IT.

ATT,
@KELLPOSKY

SCAN ME FOR COLORING GUIDE

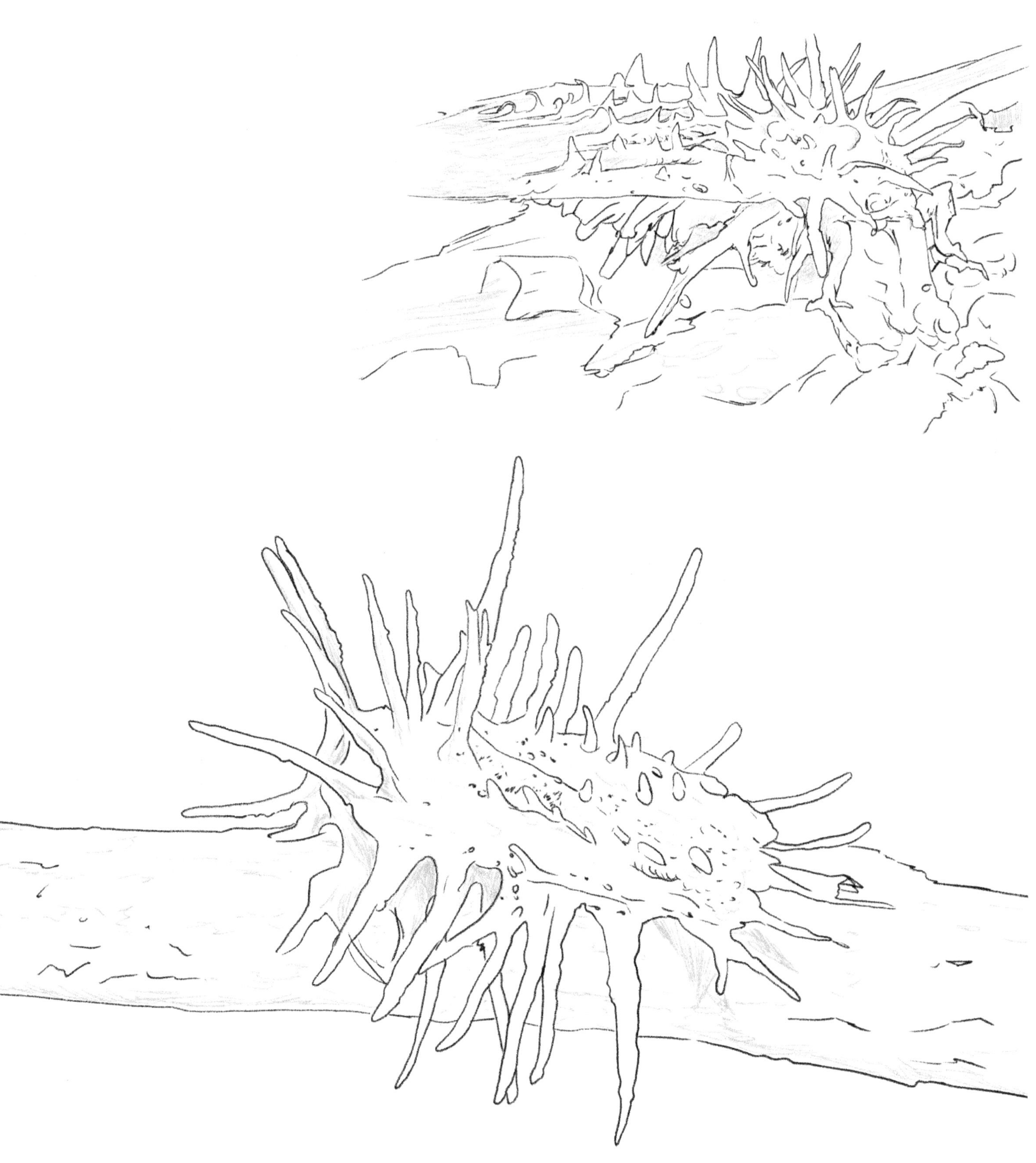

GENUS: AKANTHOMYCES SP.
ASCOMYCOTA

CORDYCIPITACEAE IS A FAMILY OF FUNGI THAT
ARE MOSTLY PARASITES OF INSECTS.
THIS FAMILY WAS FIRST PUBLISHED IN 1969 BY
MYCOLOGIST HANNS KREISEL.

THE GENUS AKANTHOMYCES HAS BEEN REPORTED
IN THE COLOMBIAN AMAZON.

GENUS: COOKEINA SPECIOSA

IN PLACES LIKE MALAYSIA THEY USE THEM AS FOOD. THIS GENUS, ALSO CALLED ROSE CUP, GROWS ON TRUNKS AND BRANCHES OF DECAYING WOOD AND IS TYPICAL OF TROPICAL AND SUBTROPICAL REGIONS THROUGHOUT THE WORLD.

THE GENUS COOKEINA SPECIOSA HAS BEEN REPORTED IN THE COLOMBIAN AMAZON.

COOKEINA SPECIOSA
COLLAGE

INSPIRED BY THIS FAMILY
I CREATED A COLLAGE.

YOU CAN SEE IT IN THE FOLLOWING QR

FAMILY SARCOSCYPHACEAE

COOKEINA SPECIOSA

ALTHOUGH THE GENUS HAS BEEN REPORTED AS
EDIBLE IN COLOMBIA, ITS USE IS NOT KNOWN. IT HAS
BEEN RECORDED THAT THE PEOPLE
PATAMONA IN GUYANA (AMAZON REGION)
USES IT AS FOOD.

FAMILY CORDYCIPITACEAE

GENUS: CORDYCEPS
SPIDER

IF A FUNGUS OF THE GENUS CORDYCEPS IS INTRODUCED
INTO AN INSECT, THE MYCELIUM INVADES IT AND ENDS
UP REPLACING THE HOST'S TISSUES, WHILE THE
FRUITING BODY (WHAT GROWS OUT OF THE INSECT)
TAKES ON VARIOUS FORMS:
CYLINDRICAL, BRANCHED OR IN SOME CASES
COMPLEX SHAPES.

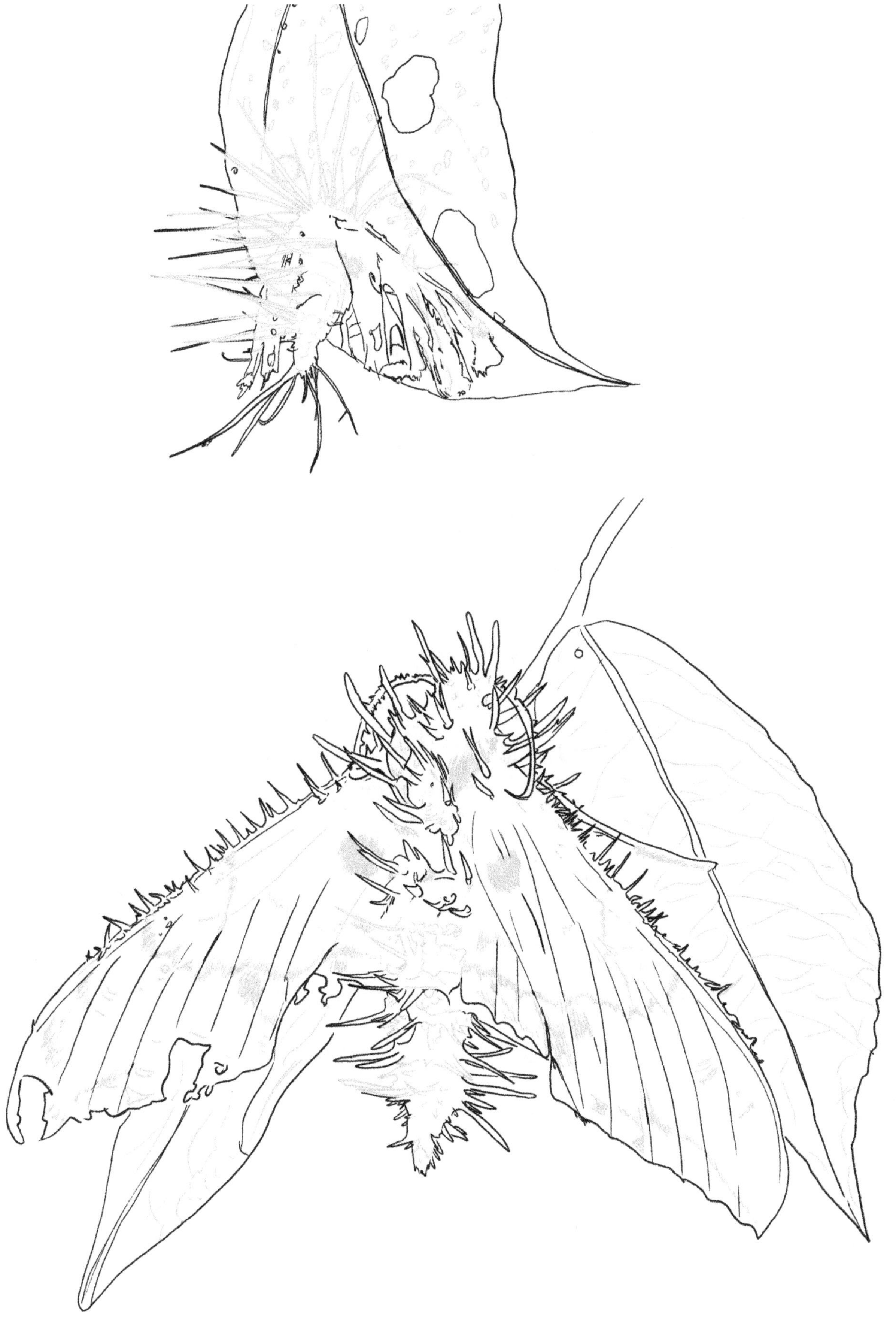

GENUS: AKANTHOMYCES TUBERCULATUS

THE CORDYCEPS FAMILY IS ABUNDANT
IN TROPICAL FORESTS .

SOME SPECIES OF CORDYCEPS ARE CURRENTLY USED
AS BIOCHEMICAL SUBSTANCES BECAUSE OF THEIR
PHARMACOLOGICAL PROPERTIES DISCOVERED AFTER
STUDIES, SOME USE CASES ARE ORGAN
TRANSPLANT SURGERIES.

FAMILY CORDYCIPITACEAE

GENUS: CORDYCEPS ANT

IN THE CASE OF CORDYCEPS ANT, THE FUNGUS HAS
THE ABILITY TO AFFECT THE BEHAVIOR OF ITS HOST
INSECT AND THAT IS WHY IT IS A GENUS.
POPULARLY CALLED ZOMBIE.

THIS FUNGUS ALTERS THE ANT'S USUAL BEHAVIOR AND
MAKES IT CLIMB TO THE HIGHEST AND FURTHEST PART
OF A PLANT BEFORE DYING, THEN RELEASES THE
SPORES FROM THE CORPSE.

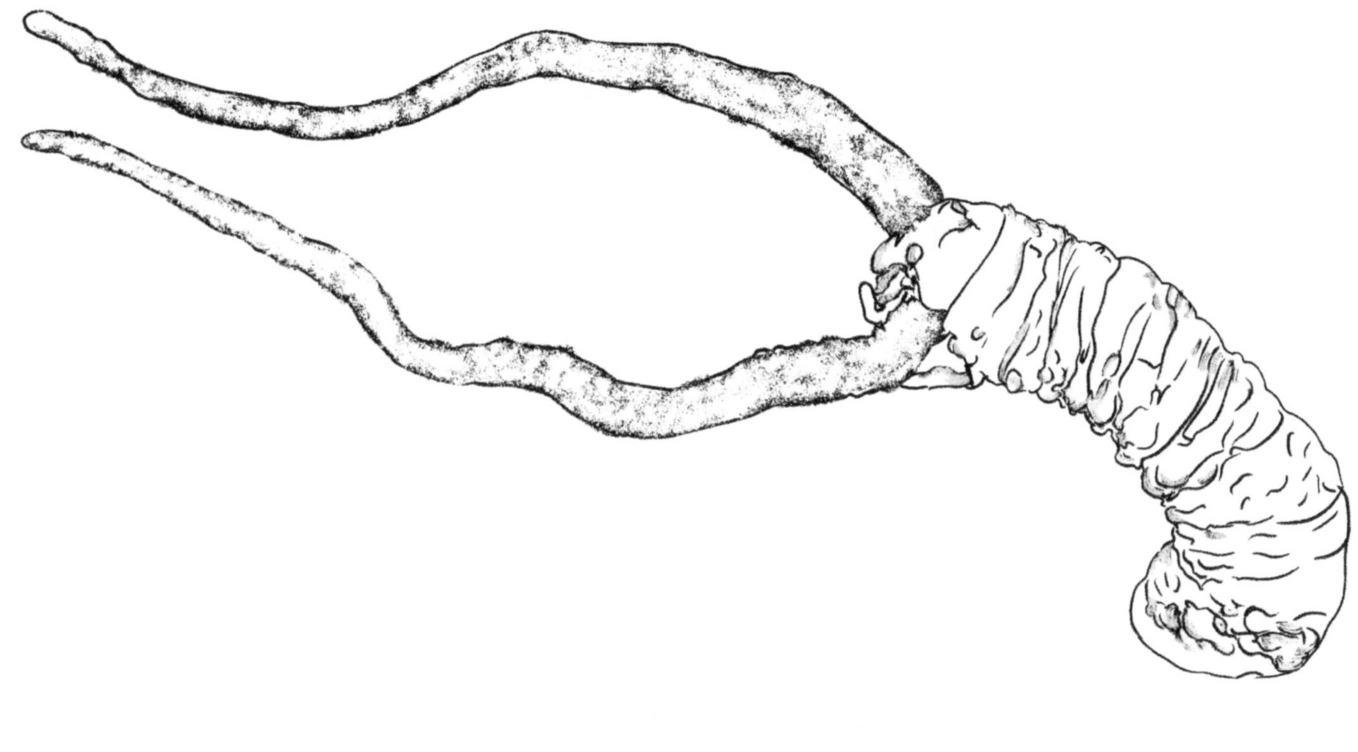

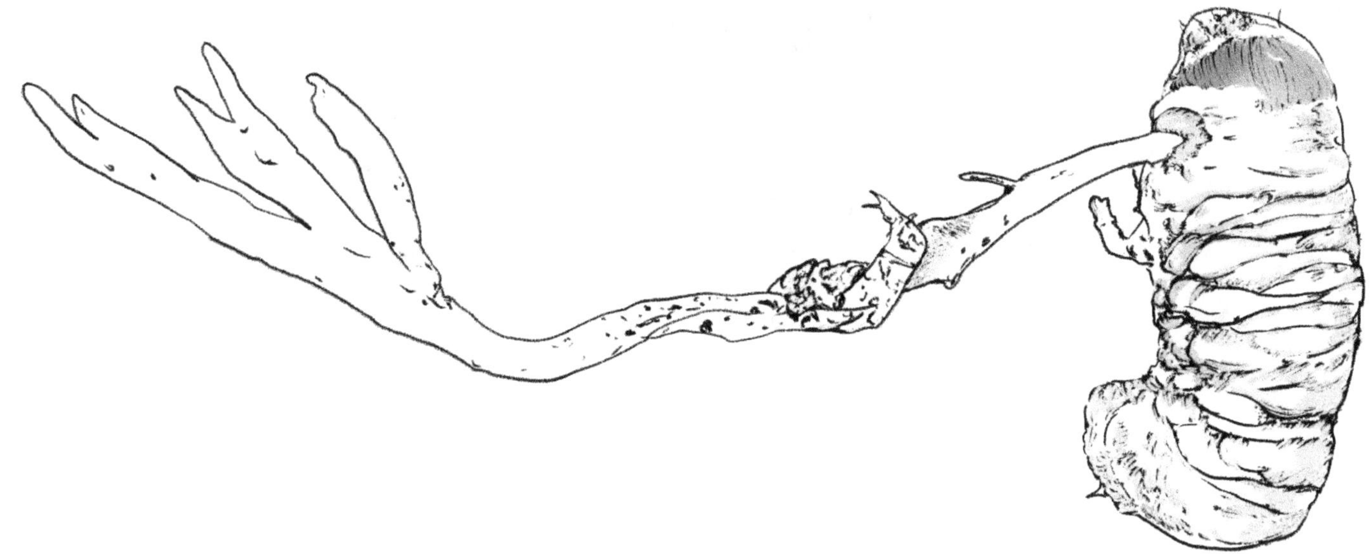

GENUS: CORDYCEPS TAKAOMONTANA

THE MYTH: IT IS SAID THAT THE EMPEROR
ZONG CHAO (IN CHINA) USED IT SEEKING VITALITY
AND LONGEVITY.

THE GENUS CORDYCEPS IN CHINESE PHILOSOPHY
PROMOTED BALANCE BETWEEN BODY AND SOUL,
WHICH IS WHY ITS CONSUMPTION WAS RECOMMENDED
TO RECOVER THE HARMONY OF THE ORGANS
OF THE BODY AND THE BALANCE OF THE SOUL.

GENUS: CORDYCEPS
BEETLE GRUB

THIS FUNGUS CAN HAVE A CYCLE
LIFESPAN OF UP TO THREE YEARS, WHICH MAKES
THIS TYPE OF PARASITIC FUNGI ARE RARE
TO DETECT. THE FUNGUS BEGINS TO GROW
AND EXITS THE HOST'S BODY THROUGH
THEIR EYES.

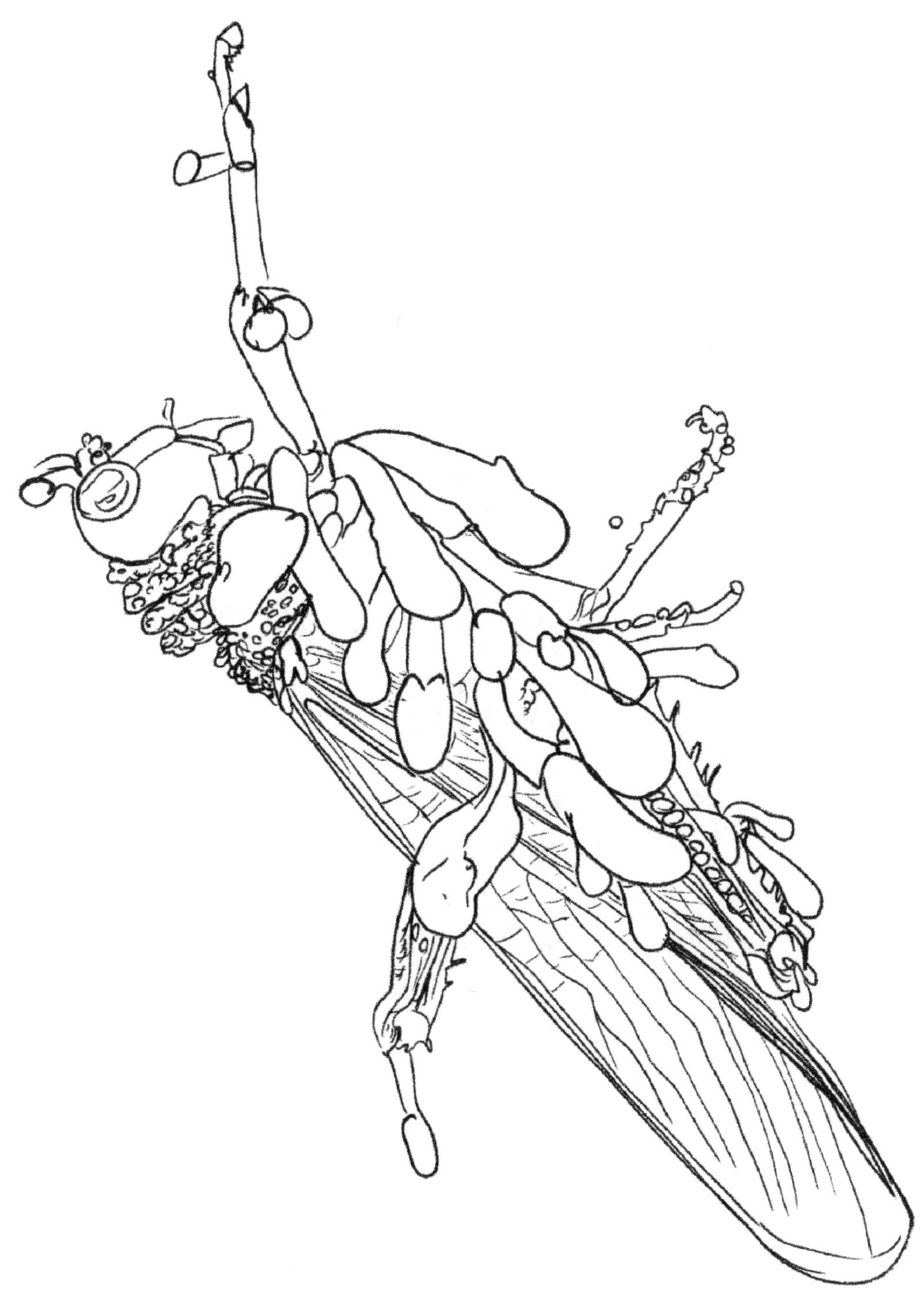

GENUS: CORDYCEPS LOCUSTIPHILA

IT IS A SPECIES OF SPECIFIC SCIENTIFIC INTEREST DUE TO ITS CAPABILITIES AS AN ENTOMOPATHOGEN.

C. LOCUSTIPHILA DOES NOT POSE A THREAT TO HUMANS, BUT THE LOCUSTS IT TARGETS CAN POSE SERIOUS THREATS TO HUMAN AGRICULTURE AND CAUSE FAMINE IN SOUTH AMERICA.

GENUS: MACROLEPIOTA
LECHUCITA

THIS SPECIES HAS A NEOTROPICAL DISTRIBUTION AND IS FOUND IN MEXICO, COSTA RICA, PANAMA, COLOMBIA AND BRAZIL, WHERE IT IS USUALLY FOUND AT ALTITUDES BETWEEN 1700 AND 3000 METERS.

IT IS A SPECIES THAT GROWS MOSTLY IN PASTURES. IT IS EDIBLE AND USED BY RURAL COMMUNITIES IN SEVERAL DEPARTMENTS OF COLOMBIA.

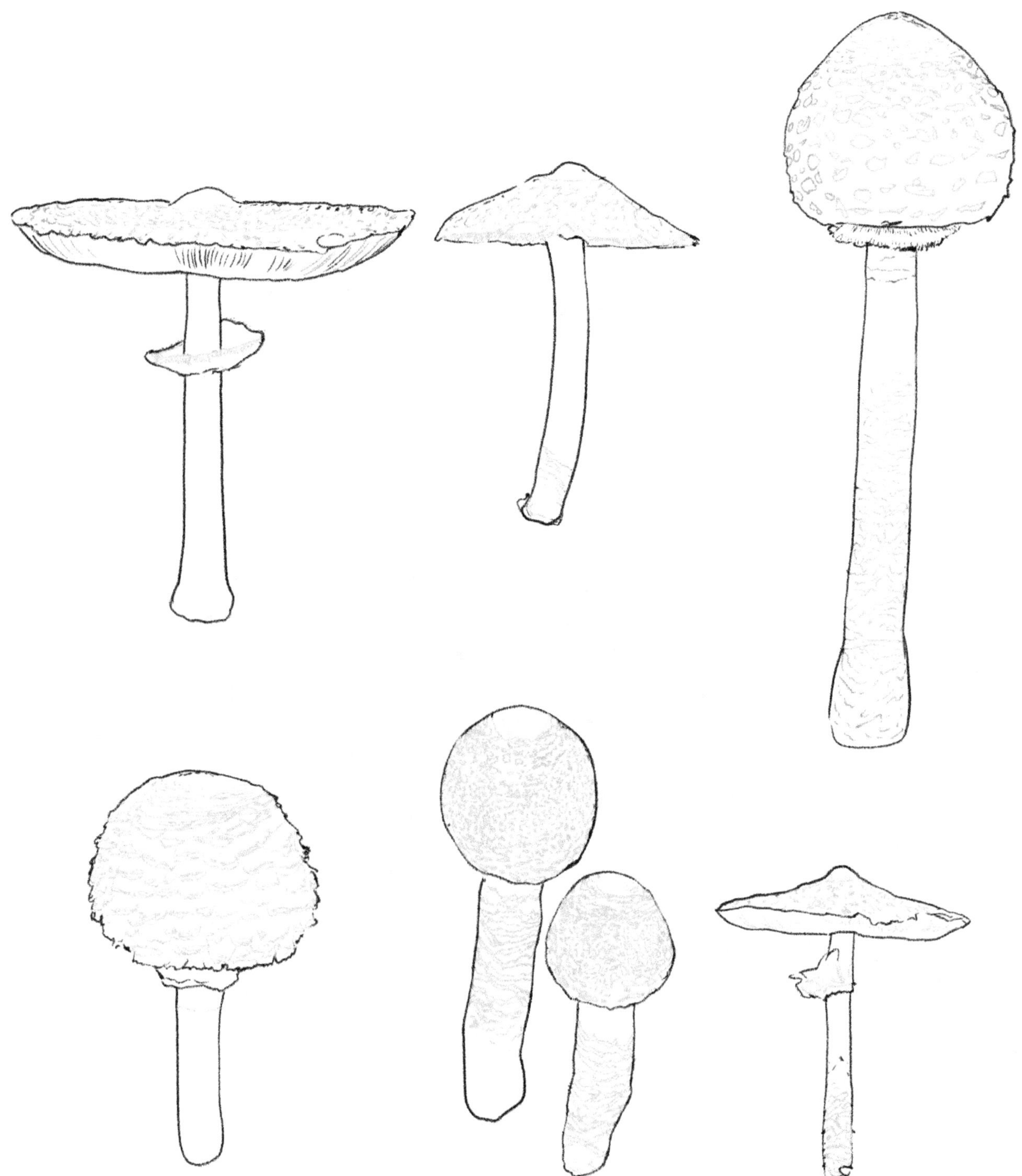

FAMILY AGARICACEAE

GENUS: MACROLEPIOTA
LECHUCITA

THE BEST KNOWN SPECIES OR TYPE IS MACROLEPIOTA PROCERA. THE GENUS HAS A VERY WIDE DISTRIBUTION AND CONTAINS ABOUT 30 SPECIES THAT ARE FOUND ALL OVER THE WORLD.

LECHUCITA COLLAGE

NOT ALL MACROLEPIOTAS ARE EDIBLE.

FAMILY GRAPHOSTROMATACEAE

GENUS: CAMILLEA LEPRIEURII

THE GENUS CAMILLEA IS DISTRIBUTED
ESPECIALLY IN TROPICAL AREAS AND IN THEIR
TAXONOMY THEY USUALLY HAVE A CYLINDRICAL SHAPE.

NO RECORD FOUND ABOUT ANY CURRENT USE
AS EDIBLE OR MEDICINAL.

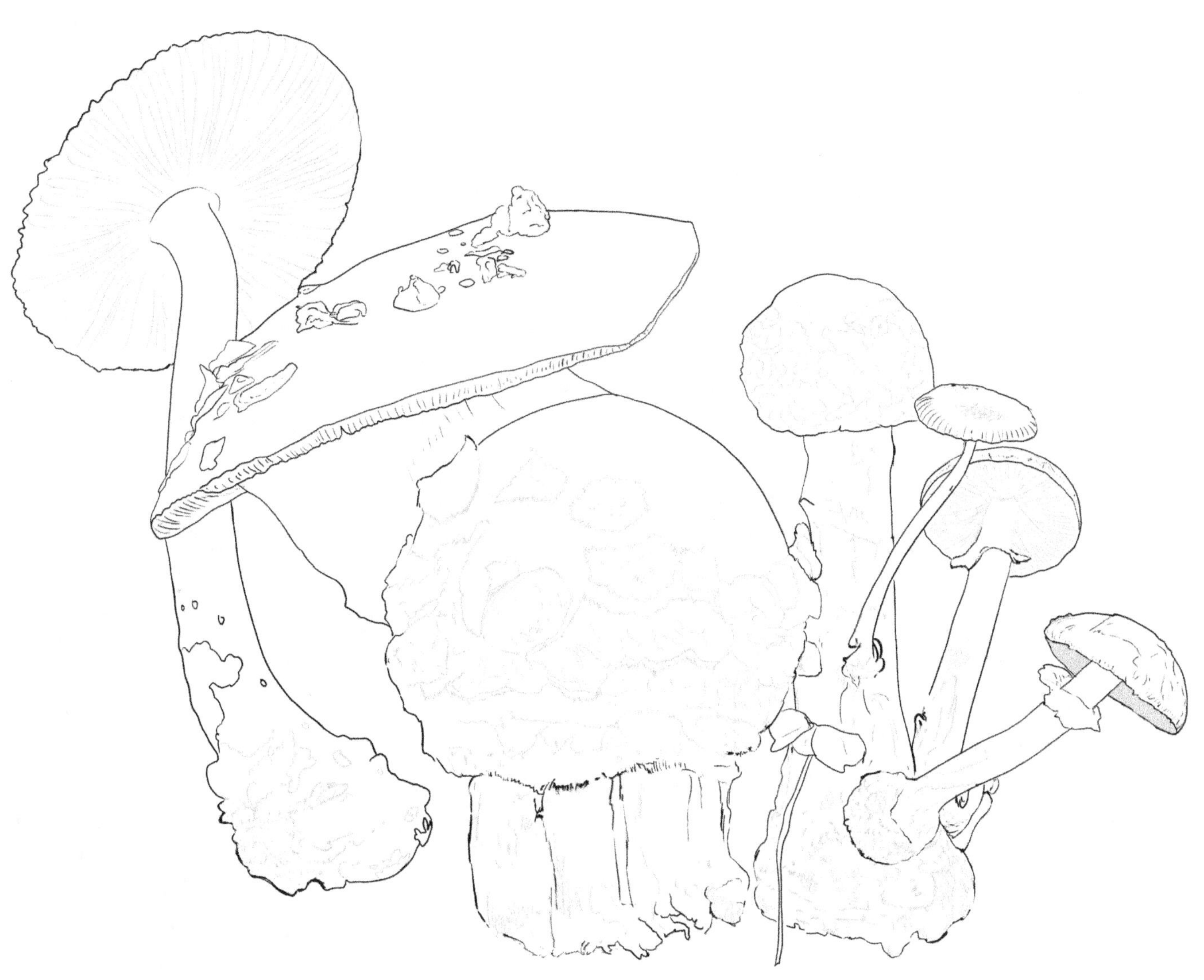

FAMILY AMANITACEAE

GENUS: AMANITA

THE GENUS INCLUDES UP TO 600 SPECIES
REGISTERED, WHICH INCLUDES EDIBLES, MEDICINALS
AND OTHERS WITH LETHAL TOXICITY.

FAMILY AMANITACEAE

GENUS: AMANITA

IN THIS GENUS WE FIND FLY AGARIC, ALSO KNOWN
AS FLY SWATTER.

IN ANCIENT TIMES IT WAS ASSOCIATED WITH
BEELZEBUB KNOWN AS THE LORD OF THE MOCHAS
AND IT WAS BELIEVED THAT ITS CONSUMPTION
CAUSED MADNESS.

AMANITA COLLAGE

TO THIS DAY THE AMANITA PHALLOIDES IS
CONSIDERED THE MOST LETHAL.

INSPIRED BY THIS FAMILY
I CREATED A COLLAGE.

YOU CAN SEE IT IN THE FOLLOWING QR

FAMILY XYLARIACEAE

GENUS: XYLARIA

THIS GENUS GROWS MOSTLY ON WOOD, BUT CAN BE FOUND IN ANIMAL MANURE, AND LEAF LITTER ON THE GROUND.

IT LIKES TO LIVE IN TROPICAL PLANTS.

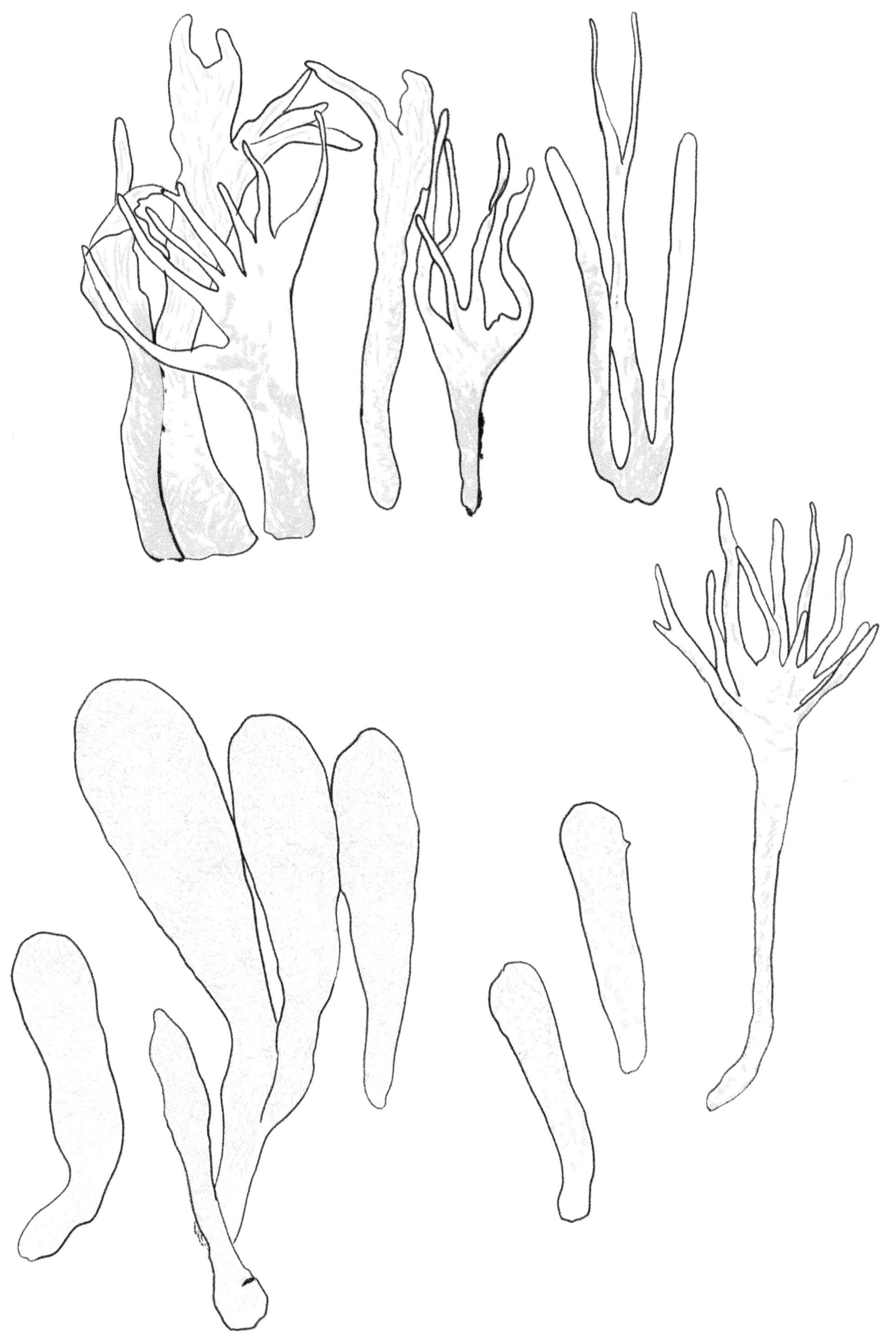

FAMILY XYLARIACEAE

FAMILY XYLARIACEAE

GENUS: XYLARIA

THE GENUS XYLARIA ENCOMPASSES AROUND 100
SPECIES AND MANY OF THEM LOOK LIKE CHARCOAL,
SOME GROW ON WOOD AND APPEARS TO BE
BURNT WOOD.

XYLARIA COLLAGE

THIS GENUS IS COMMONLY CALLED FINGERS OF
THE DEAD BECAUSE IT GROWS IN THIN CLUSTERS
THAT LOOK LIKE FINGERS.
THEY EMERGE FROM THE BASE OF A TRUNK
OR A PIECE OF WOOD.

PHALLACEAE FAMILY

GENUS: CLATHRUS
ARCHERI

THEY GROW UNDERGROUND FEEDING ON WOOD
AND WHEN THE TIME COMES TO REPRODUCE, THEY
SPROUT LIKE LIVING DEAD FROM THE GROUND, WITH
THEIR RED, VISCID AND TERRIFYING TENTACLES.

THIS MODE OF REPRODUCTION HAS MADE THIS
FUNGUS COMMONLY KNOWN AS:
"FINGERS OF THE DEVIL."

GENUS: CLATHRUS
ARCHERI

ITS SPORE CARRIERS ARE FLIES.
THEY ATTRACT THEM BY RELEASING A BLACK VISCOUS
SUBSTANCE WITH A STRONG ROTTEN SMELL.

THE FLY LANDS ON THE SUBSTANCE AND WITH LUCK IT
WILL LAND ON A LOG WHERE THE FUNGUS
IT WILL FIND ITS IDEAL HABITAT TO GROW AGAIN.

PHALLACEAE FAMILY

CLATHRUS ARCHERI
COLLAGE

THIS FUNGUS IS FOUND IN HUMID FORESTS, IN AREAS
NEAR RIVERS AND MEADOWS.

INSPIRED BY THIS FAMILY
I CREATED A COLLAGE.

YOU CAN SEE IT IN THE FOLLOWING QR

DIGITAL CAT'S TERRARRIUM

THE DIGITAL TERRARIUM FOR CATS IS A FICTIONAL PREMISE THAT I USE ON SOCIAL NETWORKS TO TALK ABOUT NATURE, THE FUNGI KINGDOM AND THE TOPICS THAT INTRIGUE ME.

THE INFORMATION BEHIND EACH PAGE IS THE COLLECTION AND SYNTHESIS OF 1 YEAR OF READING AND SEARCHING ABOUT THESE MUSHROOMS FAMILIES, MY WAY OF STUDYING HAS BEEN THROUGH DRAWING AND THIS HAS INSPIRED ME TO WRITE THIS BOOK.

IT IS IMPORTANT FOR YOU TO KNOW THAT I AM NOT A MYCOLOGIST, NOR A BIOLOGIST, I AM REALLY A LOVER OF MUSHROOMS AND THE MYSTERIES OF NATURE. THE PROCESS OF THIS BOOK WAS A CASUAL STUDY AND SELF-TAUGHT ABOUT A KINGDOM THAT IS JUST BEING EXPLORED.

IF YOU DETECT ANY ERRORS IN THE INFORMATION OR WANT TO SHARE SOMETHING ON THE TOPIC, DO NOT HESITATE TO COMMENT.

YOU CAN FIND ME ON INSTAGRAM AS @KELLPOSKY THERE I USUALLY PUBLISH MORE IMAGES AND IDEAS ABOUT THE DIGITAL TERRARIUM FOR CATS.

THANK YOU FOR YOUR PURCHASE AND CURIOSITY, IF YOU WANT MORE INFORMATION SCAN THE QR

DREAM 1